Pelargoniums

MIA ESSER

 **REBO**
PRODUCTIONS

Introduction

It is more than fifteen years since my daughter and I first visited a geraniummarket at Hilversum in The Netherlands. We were looking for frosthardy geraniums and, though I had never visited that kind of market before, I had a vague suspicion that we would not find a single fully hardy geranium. Why did we go anyway? Oh well …

Our suspicions were confirmed as soon as we arrived. There were rows upon rows of red, pink, white, upright and trailing potted geraniums, the same varieties on every stall. Even if I had wanted to buy some, which stall should I have chosen? I could not see any difference between all those plants on all those stalls, and so I would be obliged to choose a salesman instead, the jolliest one maybe. Or perhaps the one with a more creative approach, who had included some lobelias and Busy Lizzies in his display.

At the end of a long line of stalls there was one where the colours seemed a little more subdued. The trestle table was covered with tiny green cuttings interspersed with a few leaflets on the care of Pelargoniums and on the Dutch Pelargonium and Geranium Society.

What really attracted my attention was a basket crammed with a kind of purplish-pink pansies at one end of the stall. I fell in love with them straight away and tried to buy the basket. The name of the plants turned out to be Pelargonium 'Kerlander', and, no, the basket was not for sale, and the cuttings had all been sold long ago. But did I know that there were many more special pelargoniums? Within five minutes I had learnt that the nonhardy geranium was really called Pelargonium, and that thousands of different varieties were now cultivated. I returned home with four cuttings: a scented-leafed 'Lemon Queen', the Stellar 'Arctic Star', the Deacon 'Picotee', and a fancy-leafed Pelargonium called 'Rosetta'. Three months later, all the cuttings had grown into flowering plants, and I was hooked.

The pansy-flowered 'Kerlander' was one of the first plants I began to look for, and I soon realized that there were all kinds of varieties and colours. Nowadays they are readily available – most garden centres have an extensive selection in spring. There are so many special kinds that you could create an attractive and varied garden simply by filling it with plants belonging to the genus Pelargonium.

There is a huge choice varying from large plants with sizeable leaves to small succulent specimens with tiny flowers. In between those extremes, there are all kinds of leaf and flower shapes in the most diverse colours – bright yellow and blue being the sole exceptions. I hope that my account and, above all, Nico Vermeulen's magnificent photographs will encourage you to find out more about pelargoniums.

Left: Angel ' Velvet Duet' with flowers like pansies.

CHAPTER I

What is a *Pelargonium*?

Pelargoniums originally came from Cape Province in South Africa. They are commonly known as geraniums, and are among the most popular potted plants. If you visit a garden centre in spring, you will find that the display of bedding plants includes trays full of upright and trailing geraniums, the name normally used for sales purposes. Around the time of Mothering Sunday, flower shops are full of scented-leafed pelargoniums, but the assistants might not even know what you meant if you asked for one by that name.

There are, of course, genuine geraniums as well. They are found in the northern hemisphere and are winter hardy in countries like Britain and The Netherlands. For a long time, these lovely garden plants had almost disappeared, perhaps because the name suggested an annual which would have to be taken indoors every winter. More recently, however, genuine geraniums have attracted more interest and several English books have been devoted to this single genus.

They are often given titles such as 'Hardy Geraniums' to distinguish them from those other 'geraniums'.

A classical red upright pelargonium.

'Lakis' is a regal pelargonium.

Perhaps we should not worry too much about the name. After all, we tend to ask for African marigolds and Busy Lizzies instead of *Tagetes* and *Impatiens* when we visit a garden centre. When it was decided to call our Cape plant *Pelargonium* two hundred years ago, it was already widely distributed and popular under the name of geranium. A muchloved plant

Pelargonium peltatum *clambering through* Phoenix canariense.

needs a familiar name, one we do not really like to change.

The Family

Both the *Pelargonium* and the *Geranium* belong to the family of *Geraniaceae* which so far includes five genera: *Pelargonium, Geranium, Erodium, Sarcocaulon,* and *Monsonia.* One characteristic that all these genera have in common is the fruit resembling a bird's beak. The little capsule containing the seeds is supposed to represent the bird's head, and has a long beaklike point attached to it. The three genera listed below owe their names to these fruits.
- *Pelargonium* is derived from the Greek words *pelargos,* which means stork.
- *Geranium* comes from the Greek word *geranos* meaning crane.
- *Erodium* comes from the word *erodos,* which is Greek for heron.

The *pelargonium* is therefore named after the stork. The common English name for *Geranium* is cranesbill, but the Dutch one, confusingly, is storksbill (ooievaarsbek)!

Origins

The *Pelargonium* is a typical South African plant. Of the approximately 230 species known at present, 200 are found in South Africa, 18 in other parts of Africa, 2 in Madagascar, 2 in Asia Minor, and one each in Tristan da Cunha and Saint Helena. The plants like a subtropical climate.

The pelargoniums planted out around the Mediterranean appear to be capable of holding their own, but on the whole they prefer their native habitat.

Pelargonium abrotanifolium 'Naudesnek' – the fruit shaped like a stork's bill is visible in the centre of the photograph.

The scented-leafed 'Rober Lemon'.

Most of the native South African species are found in the extreme south-west of the continent, in the vicinity of the Cape of Good Hope.

On their way to Europe

As a seafaring nation, the Dutch always played a major part in bringing plants from exotic parts of the world to Europe. On their voyages to the Far East, ships anchored in the Bay of Good Hope to take on provisions and, above all, fresh drinking water. The passengers always included a few plant lovers, who used the delay to collect plants and, in particular, seeds to take back with them. Travelling home with actual plants was often more difficult. The journey was a long one, and water was usually in short supply on board. Pelargoniums, however, included many succulent plants capable of withstanding long periods of drought, and so, eventually, entire plants were shipped to Europe. The first *Pelargonium* reached Europe as a result of the efforts of an Englishman, John de Tradescant. He had collected a lot of seeds, and one of them grew into a plant which was described in 1633 as a 'Geranium indicum noctu odoratum', a nightscented geranium from India.

We now know that this was *Pelargonium triste* and had come from South Africa, not India. The plant has large, deeply divided, hairy leaves and flowers with a nutmeg fragrance in the evening.

Adriaan van der Stel, Governor of the Cape from 1699 to 1706, was a Dutchman who sent many Cape plants to Europe. Those that he dispatched to The Netherlands included *Pelargonium peltatum* and *Pelargonium zonale*, the ancestors of most of the pelargoniums available at garden centres and nurseries today.

Pelargonium cucullatum, one of the ancestors of Regal pelargoniums, was taken to the Netherlands by the botanist Paul Hermann. All those plants, seeds, and cuttings brought home by merchants and botanists found their way to botanical gardens, royal palaces, and the country houses of wealthy landowners and merchants.

Botanists wrote descriptions of the plants they had discovered, and commissioned artists to illustrate their texts with drawings. The libraries of some of the present-day botanical gardens contain several of the old books that tell us so much about the absorbing history of the *Pelargonium.*

By the end of the eighteenth century it was clear that pelargoniums were easy to hybridize and that it was possible to cultivate varieties which

Pelargonium triste, *the first species to reach Europe.*

Pelargonium *'Bella Notte' is a variety which does not resemble the wild species in any way.*

differed considerably from the wild plants collected previously. In the meantime, it had also been found that glass could be used to overwinter plants that were not fully hardy. When the British gained control of the Cape in 1802, vast quantities of plants were dispatched to Britain. After 150 years of planthunting, the Hortus Kewensis included several species of *Pelargonium* in its Catalogue No. 102. Over the next 150 years, thousands of different varieties were to find their way to the collections of enthusiasts.

'Bernardo', 'Maspalomas', and 'Blanche Roche' are cultivars of Pelargonium peltatum.

Cultivars of P. Zonale *at the foot of a wall.*

CHAPTER 2

The original Species

The approximately 200 species of native South African pelargoniums grow in a broad coastal strip from Namibia in the West to Mozambique in the East. About eighty per cent of those species are found in just a small section of that coastal strip in the extreme south-western part of the continent.

Pelargonium capitatum *is a shrub which may grow about 1m (3ft) tall and is found in regions where there may be some rainfall in summer.*

Pelargonium pulchellum, *which grows in winter.*

Conditions

Pelargoniums like a moderate, frostfree climate, and a growing season that is moist without being excessively wet. These conditions occur in the south-western regions of Cape Province in winter. Summers, however, are often hot and, above all, dry in that area, and anyone searching for pelargoniums without specialized knowledge is unlikely to find any. Many plants will have retreated underground, or will be waiting for better times after shedding their leaves.

The whole countryside will turn green again in autumn, when the cooler weather will also bring some rain. Most of the regions with summer rainfall, or where showers may occur throughout the year, are in southern and eastern South Africa. Pelargoniums found there are larger and bushier than elsewhere, and easier

for us to recognize. These species can also grow and flower out of doors in countries like Britain and The Netherlands.

Diversity

There are huge differences in the external characteristics of pelargoniums. If you look at a random selection of original species, it is hard to believe that they all belong to a single genus. There are, for instance, tuberous species visible only during the growing season, when they produce a rosette of leaves, but there are also pelargoniums with thick, succulent stems. There are bushes which grow over one metre (3 ft) tall, and species with long, prostrate stems. There are also striking differences in leaf shapes. The familiar kidneyshaped leaf occurs in a few

In the wild, Pelargonium bowkerii *produces flowers on bare stems in early spring. In a greenhouse, flowers and leaves sometimes develop simultaneously.*

Pelargonium appendiculatum *has an undergound tuber, and a rosette of leaves above ground.*

Right: Pelargonium carnosum *grows 60cm (24in) tall, and has thick, succulent stems.*

species only, and the same applies to the ivylike leaves of trailing pelargoniums. In fact, it is only possible to tell by the flowers that what you see is a pelargonium, since all of them have a spur, or nectary. Delphiniums are among the flowers with similar spurs, but in the case of pelargoniums they have become fused with the stems. If you look at a flower stem, you will see a kink marking the end of the spur just below the flower head.

The Fruit

The fruit is beakshaped, like that of all members of the *Geraniaceae* family. The five seeds are contained in a small capsule and joined to the end of the 'beak' by a style. As the fruit ripens, the middle section of the beak swells and the style is subjected to tension, which makes it

Pelargonium patulum *is an evergreen, bushy plant with lobed* *leaves.*   Right: Pelargonium ovale.

drag the seeds out of the capsule. The style then rolls itself up into a spiral. It is covered in tiny silvercoloured feathers and its tip remains attached to the end of the beak for a little longer until it is wafted away in the breeze.

When cultivated, Pelargonium ionidiflorum *bears a profusion of small flowers nearly all year round.*

The Sections

The huge diversity of pelargoniums did not make it easy to classify and name individual plants. William H. Sonder, the botanist who wrote the Flora Capensis in association with O.W. Sonder in 1842, named over 160 species of *Pelargonium* in that book. To gain some grip on the matter, he divided the plants into 15 sections on the basis of a number of external features.

Another botanist, R. Knuth, retained this classification into 15 sections in 1912, when he described the results of a study of the entire geranium family in Engler's series entitled *Das Pflanzenreich* (The World of Plants). The 15 sections are still used as a startingpoint in the ongoing research programme on pelargoniums at Stellenbosch University in South Africa.

Modern research methods have led to fresh understanding, and the 15 sections have been

reduced to 13. The research team led by Professor J.J.A. van der Walt, however, have commented that, on the whole, the classification established in 1842 corresponds remarkably well to the natural grouping of the genus.

A Selection from the various Species

The final part of this chapter is devoted to a description of individual plants from each of the sections, and will provide some more information on the great diversity of external features characteristic of the various species of wild pelargonium.

Section *Campylia*
Pelargonium ovale (see p.17) is a lowgrowing bush about 30cm (12in) tall. Its spread may be

Ivy-leafed pelargoniums 'Rouletta', 'Ville de Paris', and 'Blanche Roche'.

double its height as it is propagated by suckering shoots. The plant has grey, oval leaves, densely covered in small hairs, and pink flowers with large, slightly overlapping upper petals about 3cm (1¼in) in diameter. If well cared for, *P. ovale* may flower from February to

Pelargonium 'Splendide'.

Cultivars of Pelargonium peltatum.

October. The plants belonging to the section *Campylia* have extensive root systems which usually occupy more space than the part of the plant visible above ground. This characteristic enables the plants to survive hot, dry summers in sandy soil.

Ivy-leafed pelargoniums at the foot of a banana plantation.

Pelargonium laevigatum.

The section has produced a very lovely hybrid, *Pelargonium* 'Splendide', a seedling of *P. tricolor* x *P. ovale.* This hybrid has tricoloured flowers and leaves with grey hairs. The upper petals are winered with a blotch that is almost black; the lower petals are white. The plant flowers from February to September.

Nearly everyone admires this pelargonium, but, without a greenhouse, *P.* 'Splendide' and the other plants in this section are difficult to keep alive. They need a cool, frostfree, very light situation in winter (preferably in the upper part of a greenhouse just below the window). The plants may be moved out of doors in summer, but need to be sheltered from hot afternoon sun.

The potting compost should be freedraining and slightly acid. The plants should be watered regularly throughout the year, but only when the compost has dried out completely. Watering in a cold greenhouse in winter is a risky business – if

Above: Pelargonium inquinans.

the plants remain wet for too long, they will die. If possible, wait until the sun is shining into the building. From February until the end of the flowering season, the plants should also be given plant food containing very little nitrogen. Repotting is best done at the end of a short rest period in late September or early October, after which the plants begin to grow again.

Although not easy to manage, the plants belonging to the section *Campylia* are well worth cultivating, since nearly all of them bear lovely flowers.

Section *Ciconium*

Pelargonium inquinans is shrubby plant which may grow up to 80cm (32in) tall. The young stems are soft and pale green, and become woody as they age. The plant produces soft, rounded, lobed green leaves and large umbels of

Below: Pelargonium peltatum.

Ivy-leafed pelargonium.

um grow along the entire coast of South Africa, from the south-west to the extreme east. They continue northwards through Natal and Transvaal as far as the Yemen. The greatest variety is found in the eastern part of Cape Province, where there is some rainfall in summer.

All the plants are herbaceous bushes with thin, succulent stems.

The plants in this section are easy to manage. The rules for managing common upright and trailing pelargoniums described in the chapter on cultivation also apply to these wild species.

Section *Cortusina*

This section comprises two groups of pelargoniums. The first group consists of small, bushy plants native to the dry regions in the eastern part of South Africa, where there is some rainfall in summer. *Pelargonium odoratissimum,*

Pelargonium 'Claudius', a dwarf among commonor-garden pelargoniums.

red or orange-red flowers (some have pink and white flowers). Each umbel may bear 20 to 30 florets. I once saw *P. inquinans* attached to a dark green fence – 1.3m (4ft 4in) tall with countless flower heads. I could hardly stop looking at it.

Pelargonium peltatum, parent of the ivy-leafed pelargonium, is now also classified as belonging to the section *Ciconium.* This plant has long, soft, brittle stems and succulent, fivepointed leaves somewhat resembling those of ivy. The stems clambering over neighbouring shrubs may grow up to 2m (6ft) long. The flower heads, shorter than those of *P. inquinans,* bear only 2 to 8 florets each, but each one may be 5cm (2in) or more in diameter. Their colour varies from pale to deep pink.

These plants are, of course, closely resemble some of our common or garden pelargoniums, which are, in fact, descended from them. The pelargoniums belonging to the section *Ciconi-*

Pelargonium odoratissimum.

Right: Pelargonium echinatum.

with its small white flowers and delightfully applescented foliage, is one of the species belonging to this group.The plant produces short stalks with flower stems which grow longer during the flowering season.

In its natural habitat, it seeks the shade beneath shrubs. The plant is smothered in small flowers in summer, which makes it very suitable for growing in a container. Once you have smelt the scent released if you lightly touch the foliage, you will never want to be without one again. *P. odoratissimum* will do very well out of doors in summer, and looks lovely in a tall pot with its flower stems trailing over the rim. The plant is evergreen, and needs a frostfree, light situation in winter. A few months on the sittingroom windowsill is a possibility, but in that case you should let it acclimatize slowly, for instance by bringing it indoors as early as September before the heating is on.

Provide the plant with freedraining potting compost, regular plant food during the growing season, and water throughout the year, but only when the compost has dried out completely.

The second group consists of plants with succulent stems or underground tubers. They need these stems or tubers if they are to survive the very dry, freedraining soil along the west coast of South Africa, where there is little rainfall in winter.

Sometimes there is a dense sea mist which provides some moisture. These pelargoniums grow and flower during the winter.

The group includes *Pelargonium echinatum,* a succulentlooking plant with thorny stems which give the plant a bizarre appearance in summer, when it is leafless. The thorns consist of hardened residual stipules.

In countries like Britain and The Netherlands, *P. echinatum* begins to sprout in September, when soft green leaves appear all along its stem. In a cold greenhouse, the plant's flowering season starts in February/March and may continue until the end of June. The white or

Pelargonium domesticum 'Joy'.

Left: Pelargonium grandiflorum.

pink flowers are borne on long stems. The two upper petals have a heartshaped blotch, and the plant is sometimes called 'Sweetheart'.

If you take the plant out of doors in summer, you should stand it against an eastfacing wall or under the eaves. Water regularly while it still has leaves and flowers, but once the thorny stems are bare, you need only make sure that the soil does not dry out completely. Plant *P. Echinatum* in very freedraining potting compost with some clay, and feed it occasionally during the growing season, as the compost will gradually become impoverished.

Section *Glaucophyllum*

Pelargonium grandiflorum may grow 30 to 75cm (12-30in) tall. It has a bushy shape and greengrey foliage with a dark zone. The flowers, borne throughout the summer, are large for a wild species (up to 5cm/2in in diameter). They may be white, pale to deep pink, and are sometimes even bicoloured, with red markings on their petals. The section *Glaucophyllum* also includes *Pelargonium laevigatum* var. *oxyphyllum*. This small, shrubby plant has grey leaves consisting of three long, needleshaped lobes. Its flowers, 2cm (¾ in) in diameter, are borne throughout the year. They are deep pink, and have small red markings on the two upper petals. This section contains plants with strong foliage, which is often grey. This means that the plants like sun and tolerate drought. They grow naturally in mountainous regions where summers are hot and dry, and most of the rain falls in winter. These evergreen plants flower in summer but, because of their beautiful foliage, are well worthwhile cultivating in winter as well. They would look wonderful on a windowsill but, unfortunately, need to overwinter in a cool place and cannot survive the dry heat of a radiator. It is therefore best to put them in a green-

Pelagronium laevigatum *var.* oxyphyllum.

house. The plants in this section need very well-drained potting compost, 50% of which should consist of sharp sand or grit. Do not water until the soil has dried out completely and feed them from time to time. Covering the soil with grit will keep it cool, something these plants like.

Section *Hoarea*

The pelargoniums in the section *Hoarea* have underground tubers. They have no stem and the leaf stalks emerge directly from the soil, usually in the form of a rosette.

The plants grow almost exclusively in regions with winter rainfall. Some of them disappear underground in summer; in the case of others, *Pelargonium oblongatum*, for example, a tuber, partly above ground, with a small crown of hardened petioles, marks the place where a fresh green rosette of leaves will appear at the onset of the first rains. The flower buds develop at the end of the winter. By the time the flowers have appeared in all their glory – primrose yellow, an unusual colour for a pelargonium – the plant will have shed most of its leaves again. *Pelargonium auritum* (with black flowers) and *Pelargonium fissifolium* also belong to the section *Hoarea*. The plants in this section have many different leaf shapes. *P. auritum* is an extreme example, as it produces not just one, but several leaf shapes at the same time. These plants are particularly suitable for people who like to see plants growing and flowering in their greenhouse or cool conservatory in winter. Give them some water regularly during those months. In summer, you can stack the seemingly empty pots and store them in a dry place. Some species like a little water in a saucer once a month, but you may forget about most of them until August, when they should be potted up again in freedraining fresh compost mixed with a lot of sharp sand. The first green tips will appear two or three weeks later.

Pelargonium oblongatum.

flower stems harden as they age, and end up as thorny crowns at the top of the fleshy plants. The flowers are white with red blotches and lines, and are about 2cm (¾in) in diameter.

The young shoots of *Pelargonium alternans* are soft and green, but become woody as they age. The plant has small, hairy, deeply divided leaves and white flowers with petals that are 1cm (³/₈in) long and only 3mm (¹/₈in) wide. This small shrub looks its best in late summer when numerous flowers have appeared and the leaves are just beginning to form. The white, star-shaped flowers show up beautifully against the old, almost blackened stems.

The section *Otidia* includes plants that have adapted to drought with the aid of thick, suc-

Left: Pelargonium alternans.

Below: The hard flower stems resembling thorns remain on the plant and are a characteristic feature of Pelargonium crithmifolium.

Stellar 'Shalimar'.

culent stems used for storing water and nutrients. They also have narrow, divided leaves which restrict evaporation. The plants grow in regions where the small amount of rain falls only in winter. The largest group is found by the Orange River on the border with Namibia.

Otidias are suitable for cultivation in a frostfree greenhouse or cool conservatory. Give them welldrained soil mixed with some clay to achieve optimum results. If you also water sparingly, they will flower profusely, often twice or three times a year.

Sections *Peristera* and *Myrrhidium*

Pelargonium australe is a native Australian perennial and grows about 30cm (12in) tall. It has simple, heartshaped leaves. Branching flower stems bear umbels of small, white or pale pink florets with such short stems that they form a spherical flower head. This plant belongs to the section *Peristera*, which consists mainly of very small herbaceous plants, often with tiny flowers. In the wild, they are frequently annual because they cannot survive hot summers. When cultivated and well cared for, they will often live for several years.

The plants in this section grow naturally in a wide variety of places, including Zimbabwe, Mozambique, and Australia, as well as Tristan da Cunha and Madagascar. In South Africa, they are found in dry watercourses, where they grow and flower at great speed by making use of the brief presence of water. Because they are so small, these species are rarely cultivated. Collectors' greenhouses often contain a few that are grown for such purposes as underplanting for taller plants. I have had *Pelargonium nanum*, with its tiny leaves and even smaller flowers, in my garden for years. It grows as ground cover between a few stones. Winter frosts kill the plant, but the seed appears to be hardy, as the seedlings come up in spring even after a severe winter.

Pelargoniums belonging to the section *Myrrhidium* do not look very attractive in containers,

Pelargonium australe.

Pelargonium papilionaceum.

although they often bear large flowers. They are herbaceous plants with lax stems and pinnate leaves.

In the wild, they die down during the heat of summer, and several plants can apparently survive only as seed. They grow in the wetter parts of regions with winter rainfall, and on the higher levels of areas where it rains in summer.

Section *Pelargonium*

Pelargonium papilionaceum is a tall shrub; even in a pot it may grow to about 1.5m (5½ft) in the course of a few years. The stems of this shrub grow woody and its large leaves are very fragrant. The pink flowers have two large upper petals with red markings, and three very small lower petals. The flowers, about 2cm (¾in) across, are small in proportion to the plant, but very numerous.

Papilionaceum means 'resembling a butterfly', and the name describes the flowers. The flowering season begins early, about the end of April, and continues until June. Most years, this is followed by a second flowering in August. This handsome container plant also makes a splendid foliage plant when not in flower. It grows wild in the semishade of ravines and forest margins, and will even tolerate a half-shady situation in summers like those in Britain or The Netherlands.

Pelargonium radens is one of the pelargonium species cultivated for the production of geranium oil. In the wild, this shrub may grow up to 90cm (36in) tall, but it will stop at 60cm (24in) in a pot. The stems become woody as they age, with the oldest ones eventually acquiring fine markings on their bark. The very finely divided leaves have a herby fragrance and feel feel rough to the touch. Softpink flowers are borne in small clusters of no more than six flowers, and measure about 2cm (¾in) across. If you like a profusion of flowers, it is better not to cultivate this

plant, although its lacy foliage and delicate flowers show up well in a group of container plants. The plants in this section are branching, shrubby plants with small flowers.

Pelargonium cucullatum, one of the ancestors of the regal pelargonium, is an exception to this rule. This plant bears flowers measuring as much as 5cm (2in) across. The section also includes several plants that have become known as scented-leafed pelargoniums. Although the plants in this section are found along the entire coast of South Africa, they grow most frequently in areas where some rain falls throughout the year. Most species tolerate the often damp summers of north-west Europe reasonably well. Plant them in freedraining soil

Left: Pelargonium radens.

Below: Pelargonium bowkerii.

in roomy pots, water when the potting compost feels dry to the touch, and feed regularly. In winter, they like a cool and light situation. This may cause some problems, as most species require a lot of space.

Section *Polyactium*
Pelargonium bowkerii has a large undergound tuber and, above ground, a small stem with large, very delicately divided leaves which may grow up to 40cm (16in) long. Because all the leaves are covered in small, soft, grey hairs, it makes a magnificent foliage plant. It gradually sheds its leaves in winter, and just as you are about to put it somewhere out of sight, you discover that it has flower buds.

The flowers develop in February, which is unusual for a pelargonium.They are unremarkable in colour, strawyellow or a dusty kind of pink. Their form, however, is very striking, with the five petals mostly divided into narrow lobes.

The plant grows naturally in eastern South Africa at levels varying between 1100m (3,355ft) and 2200m (6,710ft), where the rainfall may be as much as 600-800mm (24-32in) during the summer months.

In the British or Dutch climate, the plant may be moved out of doors in summer, when the leaves are at their best. Stand it among other container plants or in a conspicuous situation in the garden.

Put *Pelargonium triste* in a dark corner of the shed during the summer months, because all that is visible in the pot is a small section of the underground tuber and a few hardened remains of the previous winter's growth. The plant comes to life again in August, and then rapidly produces large, soft leaves, very finely divided like those of carrots, and sometimes covered in grey hairs.

Stellar 'Ade's Elf'

The plant has a considerable spread, because some of the leaves develop horizontally round the stem. From January onwards, the plant develops long flower stems bearing flowers which are usually purplish brown with soft yellow margins. Large cream or greenish yellow flowers are also found.

Pelargonium triste.

Nearly all the flowers in the section *Polyactium* have nightscented flowers. When I walk past the greenhouse in the evening or very early in the morning during the flowering season, there is a delightful smell of nutmegs. The plants use their fragrance rather than their modest colours to entice the nocturnal insects that ensure pollination.

All these species have a tuberous root system and, unlike the plants in the section *Hoarea*, a stem above ground. The large leaves have various shapes, and the plants' growth forms and flowering seasons also differ according to the rainfall in the regions where they are found.

In dry seasons, the plants die down above ground. With their large leaves, these pelargoniums require humusrich, freedraining soil, and rather more food and water than other wild species.

Pelargonium fruticosum produces deeply divided leaves almost all year round.

Pelargonium acetosum is easy to cultivate.

The same general rule applies, though – do not water until the soil feels dry to the touch. During their leafless period, the plants need very little moisture, and on cold, damp winter days it is better not to water until there has been an hour or two of sunshine.

Cultivating wild species

One of the interesting aspects of cultivating these original pelargoniums is that an assortment of species from the various sections will provide you with a wide range of plants which, to your surprise, all belong to the same genus. Because the various species have different growing and flowering seasons, you can have flowering plants in your greenhouse or garden throughout the year.

In our climate, Pelargonium pulverulentum *begins to sprout in August and flowers in a greenhouse in winter.*

A frostfree greenhouse is almost essential for overwintering and propagating botanical species.

The plants, however, do require some attention both in summer and in winter. To achieve good results when cultivating these original species, you will need more information than can be provided in this book. If you are interested, try out a few easy species first. Once you have gained some experience with succulent plants, you will soon be able to progress to more difficult species.

You can also join a Pelargonium Society. There are several international and national societies which study this genus – not including the cultivated species – in greater depth.

Propagation

Buying wild species of pelargonium is not very easy. There are relatively few specialized growers, but it is sometimes possible to acquire plants from members of a Pelargonium Society.

Propagation is not always easy. If you want to propagate your plants yourself, it is easiest to do so with plants belonging either to the section *Ciconium* or to the section *Pelargonium.* You can take cuttings from these plants in the same way as described for cultivars in the chapter on cultivation. Plants from the section *Polyactium* are also relatively easy to propagate, and that is also true of the plants in the sections *Cortusina* or *Ligularia* that form small underground tubercles. Break off a tubercle and plant it in a pot, making sure that the side originally attached to the root system faces upwards. Cover it with compost until it is buried just below the surface and keep the potting compost slightly moist. At a temperature of 15-20°C (59-68°F), the tubercle will begin to sprout in two or three

The tubercles of Pelargonium pulverulentum *may be used for propagation.*

Pelargonium x peltatum with 'cranesbills'. Pelargoniums hybridize very easily, so that not only the seeds of cultivars, but also those of botanical species may produce deviant plants.

Pelargonium hedges on La Palma.

weeks' time. Of course, you may also sow seeds of the original species but, because pelargoniums hybridize easily, you should only use seed from plants that have been in an isolated situation and have been pollinated by hand. Seed from plants pollinated by insects may produce hybrids. That may be intriguing, of course, but that is a different story. The remainder of this book is devoted to cultivars and spontaneously created hybrids.

Plant the tubercles the right way up.

Hybrid of Pelargonium graveolens.

Cultivars

It is impossible to consider cultivars whilst ignoring hybrids. A hybrid is the result of crosspollination, but that is not necessarily caused by human action. If two species belonging to the same plant genus grow close together in the wild, crosspollination is possible. If that leads to the creation of a plant, it is called a hybrid. Several natural pelargonium hybrids are known, but most of them were produced as a result of collectors placing various species close together in small areas. This led to the creation of hybrids that could not have developed in the wild because the various species required totally different conditions and therefore grew in areas situated far away from one another.

Pelargonium x stenopetalum, *a hybrid of* P. zonale.

The word cultivar is a combination of the words 'cultivated' and 'variety', and a cultivar is therefore a plant that has been created as a result of human action. This is usually done by crossing different species, although it is not essential. It is also possible to create a cultivar by selecting a plant with a deviant form and attempting to propagate it without losing those deviant characteristics.

Explosive Development

The first pelargonium hybrids were produced at an early stage. *Pelargonium* hybrids drawn by artists and described by botanists were named as early as the 18th century, although it was often uncertain which species had been in-

Left: 'Pink Happy Thought' was developed from a deviant shoot of 'Happy Thought'.

Pelargonium x blanfordianum, *a plant for enthusiasts.*

'Flower of Spring', a cultivar introduced in 1860.

volved in the hybridization. Some of these early hybrids still circulate in the collections of enthusiasts. Growers, with their vast knowledge of hybridization, started working on pelargoniums, first in Britain, but in the 19th century also in France and other European countries.

There was an explosive development of new cultivars, and by the mid nineteenth century as many as 6000 appear to have been described. Numerous new cultivars from America and Australia were added in the 20th century, and by the 1950s more than 10,000 pelargonium hybrids had been described. Even in the case of those more recent hybrids marketed by growers, it is not always possible to find out exactly how they were produced. And the cultivation of new varieties still continues!

Classification into Groups

Just as was done in the case of the original species, attempts were made to classify cultivars by dividing them into groups. The first systematic classification was the work of the American L.M. Bailey, who divided the pelargonium cultivars into the following groups in a book on horticulture published in 1917:

– *Pelargonium* x *hortorum* Zonal pelargoniums. *Hortorum* comes from the Latin word *hortus*, meaning garden. In other words, these plants are suitable for gardens, and are therefore bedding plants.

– *Pelargonium* x *peltatum* Ivy-leafed pelargoniums. The name is derived from the Latin word *peltatus,* which means shield. The leaves are supposed to resemble shields.

– *Pelargonium* x *domesticum* Regal pelargo-

P. 'Lilian Pottinger' bears small flowers and has a pineapple fragrance.

eighteenth century. They were prominently displayed in castles and large country houses, since flowerscented sprays to drive away obnoxious smells from people's homes had not yet been invented. In Britain, in particular, collecting this

kind of plant became all the rage among the upper classes. This vogue led to a considerable increase in the number of hybrids. Professional growers were less interested in scented-leafed plants, as the scent that would ultimately be achieved could not be predicted while the hybrids were being developed. They had also learnt from experience that the scent sometimes disappeared altogether during hybridization. Most of the scented-leafed pelargoniums are shrubby plants with small flowers. The shape, size, and colour of the leaves vary from cultivar to cultivar. Some scented-leafed plants have variegated foliage, and there are even some with large flowers. Lists of scented-leafed pelargoniums often include a number of species. These genuine species do not really belong in this book, in which the pelargoniums are introduced in groups. It often happens, though, that

P. 'Sweet Mimosa' flowers from March to November; its scent is vaguely spicy.

P. 'Chocolate Tomentosum' has soft felty leaves with a
peppermint fragrance. Its flowers are small, just like those
of Pelargonium tomentosum, from which it is descended.

P. 'Brunswick' is a sturdy plant with large flowers and a sweet,
spicy fragrance.

a plant such as *Pelargonium tomentosum*, with
its velvety leaves and strong peppermint fragrance, is regarded as a scented-leafed pelargonium rather than as a species. It is referred to as
one of the ancestors of many plants, but,
unfortunately, the influence of this unique,
agnificent plant is rarely evident. *Pelargonium
crispum* and *Pelargonium graveolens* are the
principal species from which many cultivars
have been developed. *Pelargonium odoratissimum*, with its aroma of sweet apples, should
also be mentioned here.

Cultivation

Scented-leafed pelargoniums may be kept out
of doors in full sun or semishade in summer.
Their fragrance becomes stronger in a sunny
location. Tending these scented-leafed plants on
a hot summer's day is a delightful experience.
Instructions on how to take cuttings from these
plants is described in the chapter on propagation,
but you will need rather more patience than for
other pelargoniums. It may be four to six weeks
before the cuttings develop roots. As long as the
leaves are fresh and green, there is no need to
worry about whether the cutting has been unsuc-
cessful.

How to look after scented-leafed pelargoniums
in general is described in the chapter on cultivation.

Next pages: Ivyleaf 'Pink Carnation'.

Pelargonium fulgidum is one of the ancestors of the Uniques.

Uniques

This group consists of bushy, sometimes sturdy plants with woody stems. Their blooms are borne in small flower heads and have striking colours, usually red with dark, or even black blotches and streaks. Just a few cultivars have pink, salmon-pink or white flowers. They resemble the flowers of regal pelargoniums, but the leaves are deeply and irregularly divided, and have a sharp, spicy fragrance.

History

Pelargonium fulgidum, a small, shrubby species with bright red flowers, is probably an important ancestor of the Uniques. *P.* x *domesticum* has often been used for later hybrids, and is probably responsible for their sturdy, shrubby shapes and woody stems.

The first cultivar in this group was introduced about 150 years ago under the name of 'Old

'Scarlet Pet' also belongs to the Unique group.

'Paton's Unique'.

Zonal pelargonium 'Hope Valley' has yellow-green leaves.

Unique'. Its many descendants subsequently became known as Uniques. In Victorian times, when bedding plants became fashionable, the Uniques were among the favourites. Whether the 'Old Unique' has survived is uncertain. At one time, the plant's alternative name was 'Rollison's Unique', and that name is still found in the assortment. It is a tall plant bearing purplishred flowers with dark blotchess and streaks.

Cultivation

Uniques are plants that are well able to hold their own in the wet summers of countries like Britain and The Netherlands. When a rainy summer has caused many plants to shed their blooms, the Uniques calmly go on flowering. Whether they are planted out in open ground or grouped in containers in the garden, they will bloom throughout the summer. Since the plants sometimes grow over 1m (3ft) tall, they will require a lot of space in winter. It is best to prune them hard at regular intervals, partly because the lower part of the stems tends to become rather bare. They should not, however, be cut back into the woody part of the stems. Cuttings, like those of scented-leafed pelargoniums, may take some time to develop roots, but, apart from that, Uniques are among the easiest pelargoniums to manage.

Pelargonium x *domesticum* (Regal Pelargonium)

These pelargoniums have many different names. They are called Regals in Britain, Grandiflorum hybrids in Germany, and French geraniums in the Netherlands. In France they are known as Odiers, and in America as Lady or Martha Washingtons or simply as Marthas.

The presentday regal pelargonium is a bushy plant, with stems and branches which become woody as they age. The cuplike leaves face upwards. They are heartshaped, serrated, and

Miniature zonal pelargonium 'Parmenter Pink'.

'Patricia Andrea'.

Cultivation

The cultivation of plants in this groups differs to some extent from the procedure for other pelargonium cultivars. Use ordinary potting compost, which may be mixed with a little peat, since these plants like light, slightly acid soil. Avoid excessive growth and a lack of flowers by using pots that are not too large. Water and feed regularly in spring and summer.

P. domesticum is usually bought for cultivation as an indoor plant but, because it likes a cool, dry situation, it does better out of doors, although the flowers tend to be spoilt by rain. The most suitable place for the plant would therefore be under the eaves, or against an east-facing wall. If you have enough space, it is worthwhile letting older plants overwinter, in

Right: Regal pelargonium 'Dark Secret'.

Dwarf zonal pelargonium "Clara Read'.

feel rough to the touch. The flowers are large, 5cm (2in) across, and are sometimes likened to those of petunias. There are cultivars with single or double flowers, with streaks or blotches on all petals, and sometimes with ruffled or fringed margins. Colours vary from white, pink, red and purple to almost black.

History

The principle ancestors of this group are *Pelargonium grandiflorum* (large-flowered) and *Pelargonium cucullatum. Cucullatum* means calyxshaped and refers to the plant's cup-shaped leaves. Both characteristics are found in *P.* x *domesticum.* Hybridization began in Britain as early as 1800. The plants obtained in that way were sent to the continent as English geraniums, and were used for further cultivation in France and Germany. The idea was to produce ever-larger flowers in striking shades and without blotches or streaks.

which case they grow into sturdy shrubs that may flower abundantly. If you do not want large plants, or do not have enough room to keep them, you should take cuttings in August (see chapter on propagation). As soon as the cuttings have developed roots, they should be planted in a pot with a diameter of 10cm (4in). Large plants that are to overwinter are also best repotted in autumn. Keep the plants out of doors until the first night frost, as they need a cold period if they are to flower early and abundantly the following year. About six weeks at a daytime temperature of approximzately 10°C (50°F) is enough, but remember that neither the plants nor the cuttings can tolerate night frosts. After they have had their cold period, the regals can spend the winter on a cool windowsill or in a greenhouse. Keep the plants slightly moist in winter. If managed in this way, they will flower again in early summer.

P. 'Lord Bute' is a regal pelargonium with small flowers. It dates from 1910 and is very popular nowadays.

Pelargonium x domesticum 'Fringed Aztec'.

Below: 'Beromünster' is a regal pelargonium that remains small.

Angels

The plants in this group do not grow more than about 30cm (12in) tall and have thin, woody, upright stems with small, crenated leaves surrounding, and attached to them. The upper petals are broader than the lower ones and overlap each other, which makes the flowers look rather like pansies.

In America, they are sometimes called 'Pansy-faced'. The blooms are usually soft mauve, with blotches and streaks in a darker shade. Some plants bear white, pink, or deep mauve flowers. The principal, and very profuse flowering season is in August, after which the plants continue to flower right through the summer, though a little less abundantly.

P. *x* hortorum *'Mr Wren' is a very sturdy zonal pelargonium.*

lands, they are usually called Zonal Pelargoniums in Britain, after *Pelargonium zonale*, a species with upright stems, round leaves, and large clusters of pale pink flowers. *Pelargonium inquinans*, which produces leaves of a similar

shape but without zones, is another ancestor. This sturdy plant bears heads of red, orange, pink, or white flowers. The individual florets of both plants open gradually, and so the flower heads may continue to bloom for weeks on end. The origin of the first hybrid is unknown. It was found in a botanical garden and used as basic material for the thousands of cultivars that were to follow. These upright pelargoniums, however, differed so much in appearance that it became necessary to divide them into subgroups.

Large Zonal Pelargoniums

Large zonal pelargoniums include all those that grow more than 25cm (10in) tall. Like the species from which they are descended, the oldest cultivars are sturdy plants which may grow about 70 to 80cm (28-32in) tall, and produce strong stems and foliage. It is still just possible

P. *x* hortorum *'Francis James' bears white flowers with pink centres and narrow pink margins.*

P. *x* hortorum *'Skelly's Pride' has serrated petals.*

to obtain a few of the finest nineteenth-century plants, 'King of Denmark', for instance, which bears semidouble pink flowers.

History

In 1908, the Frenchman Bruant produced 'Fiat', a strong zonal pelargonium with slightly hairy greygreen foliage and bearing a profusion of semidouble pink blooms. A whole series of these zonal pelargoniums followed, all called 'Fiat'. They were all very sturdy plants with semidouble flowers. The tales about 'geraniums' that could be lifted in autumn and rolled in newspaper to overwinter in a dark corner somewhere date back to those days. An occasional sprinkling of water was supposed to be enough to keep them from drying out completely. I do not recommend this treatment for modern pelargoniums, as most of them would

P.x hortorum 'Creamery' does not grow very tall and is difficult to cultivate.

fail to sprout again in spring. The following plants belong to the group consisting of large zonal pelargoniums.

Irenes

In 1942, the American Behringer produced the first 'Irene' from the 'Fiats'. It was named after his wife, and a whole series followed. An 'Irene' may grow up to 80cm (32in) tall. The plant bears an abundance of large, semidouble flowers throughout the summer. From 1965 onwards, other growers also began to produce hybrids from old species.

In addition to the name of the cultivar, specialized growers will always state whether the plant is an 'Irene'.

Tulip-flowered Pelargoniums

A 'Fiat' sport, an atypical form, was used to cultivate a plant with semidouble carminepink flowers shaped like unopened tulips. The American growers, Mr and Mrs Andrea, named it 'Patricia Andrea'. There are only a few tulip-flowered pelargoniums, so they cannot really be called a series. They are bizarre plants, though, and appeal strongly to flower arrangers. Tulip-flowered pelargoniums sometimes produce shoots with ordinary halfopen flowers, the reason being that these cultivars have a strong tendency to revert to their original forms. To prevent

P. x hortorum 'Jacey' with double flowers.

Tulip-flowered 'Patricia Andrea'.

announced the introduction of a pompon-flowered pelargonium. The double flowers have so many petals that they closely resemble half-open roses, hence their name. The bestknown and, in my opinion, still the most beautiful cultivar is called 'Appleblossom Rosebud' (1870). The flower heads consist of closely packed white flowers with pink margins and green centres. Although 'Appleblossom Rosebud' is regarded as one of the large zonal pelargoniums, there are also varieties that are less than 25cm (10in) tall. These plants are easy to grow on a windowsill.

that happening, the branch bearing such flowers should be cut back to its base.

Rosebuds

In 1876, the Royal Horticultural Society Journal

F1-hybrids

All the cultivars described so far can only be propagated from cuttings. As pelargoniums are subject to bacterial diseases, methods have been

'Pink Pandorra' is a tulip-flowered cultivar which produces a shoot with ordinary flowers.

'Appleblossom Rosebud' is a sturdy zonal pelargonium.

sought for propagating them from seed instead of from cuttings, which transmit such diseases. The trouble with the seeds of cultivars is that plants grown from them do not not always come true. They differ from the parent plant and also from one another. If a particular method of hybrid-

' Garnet Rosebud' is a miniature zonal pelargonium.

'Orbit Appleblossom' was grown from a packet of F1-hybrid seed.

ization is adopted, however, seeds are obtained which grow into very healthy, uniform plants. These plants are called F1-hybrids.

F1-hybrids are compact, flower abundantly, and are available in various colours at almost any garden centre, but you can also sow them yourself. Sow as early as November to ensure that you have flowering plants by the following summer.

The temperature for germination should be about 23°C (72°F), and the seedlings should subsequently be kept in a very light place. In winter, that is not a simple matter unless you have soil-heating facilities and plant lamps. The seeds are relatively expensive compared with the cost of plants in spring, and it is worth thinking twice before buying them.

'Pac Palais' is a fairly new cultivar which can withstand wind and rain.

'Bernardo' is a new French cultivar and is propagated from cuttings.

Cultivation

All the above large zonal pelargoniums demand extra attention when it comes to watering and feeding. To encourage the plants to grow well, you will need to pot them on several times at first. In summer, in the flowering season, you should water freely and give them plant food containing a lot of potassium and not much nitrogen. Nitrogen fertilizer is very suitable in early spring, when the leaves are about to develop, but if you go on with that throughout the year, you will have masses of greenery and very few flowers. Apart from that, the rules are the same as those described in the chapter on cultivation.

Dwarfs and Miniatures

Dwarf zonal pelargoniums are those which do not grow more than 25cm (10in) tall. If they are even smaller, 15cm (6in) or less, they are called

Below: 'Friesdorf' is a dwarf with dark green foliage.

'Kleine Liebling' syn. 'Petit Pierre' is an early miniature from Germany.

miniatures. Small pelargoniums are easy to overwinter in a centrallyheated house. Growers respond to this trend by using growth inhibitors, which keep the plant more compact. If you propagate such plants from cuttings, you will find that the new plants revert to their natural sizes. Growers also develop genuine dwarfs and miniatures by using existing miniatures. In 1890, 'Black Vesuvius' was produced in Britain from a sport of 'Vesuvius'. It is a splendid little plant with red flowers and dark, almost blackishgreen foliage. Not only the size of the plants themselves differs from that of the large zonal pelargoniums, but the flower heads and leaves are also smaller. Every kind of green is represented in the foliage of small zonal pelargoniums, but it is, above all, that dark green, almost black shade of the first miniature that is to be seen in many other specimens.

Below: 'Aries', a salmon-pink miniature.

Miniature 'Frills' has distinctive flowers.

Cultivation

Dwarfs and miniatures grow slowly and it is true to say of all these plants that enough and to spare is too much. The potting soil should be free-draining and consist of two parts potting compost and one part sharp sand. Use small pots – size 9 is big enough for a mature plant. Excessive amounts of water and plant food are harmful, and the plants should therefore be given half the amount recommended by the manufacturer. A winter temperature of 15ºC (59ºF) is adequate. Many of the plants can overwinter on a windowsil in a livingroom.

Deacons

Deacons may flower more profusely than any other pelargonium. Most of them are dwarfs,

Deacon 'Birthday'.

Left: this miniature zonal pelargonium 'Orion' was used with ivy-leafed 'Blue Peter' to breed the very first Deacon.

Deacon 'Peacock' has a light green blotch in the centre of its leaves.

Deacon 'Constancy'.

Deacon 'Jubilant'.

with just a few growing a little taller. The small plants branch out well as a rule, but remain neat and compact. They were developed by the English clergyman S.P. Stringer, who crossed ivy-leafed and miniature zonal pelargoniums. His aim was to cultivate pelargoniums which did not grow too big and would bear an abundance of double flowers, and he certainly proved successful!

Cactus-flowered Zonal Pelargoniums

These pelargoniums have petals that curl inwards slightly like some chrysanthemums. There is also a cactus dahlia with furled petals of that kind.

Most of these pelargoniums do not grow more than 25cm (10in) tall. This type of plant has existed since the end of the nineteenth century, but only a few of the old cultivars are in circulation. The new ones all come from America.

Stellars

Stellars are plants with starshaped leaves and flowers. The two upper petals are narrow and

Right: 'Mini Czech', a dwarf cactus-flowered pelargonium.

'Cherry' is a mediumsized, cactus-flowered zonal pelargonium.

'Star of Persia', a cactus-flowered zonal pelargonium with white blooms.

forked; they are smaller than the three lower ones, which have serrated edges. The plants grow 25 to 30cm (10-12in) tall. They were

Stellar 'Tracery'.

developed by the Australian grower Ted Both, who used a relatively unfamiliar cultivar, the Chinese cactus-flowered 'Fiery Chief', for the purpose.

The first Stellars came to Europe from Australia in the 1960s, and new kinds are still being developed. There are white, pink, and red Stellars, and also some with bicoloured single or double blooms. Many of them have leaves with a coloured blotch; others have leaves with such large zones that the brown part occupies almost the entire surface.

Bird's Eggs

These zonal pelargoniums are so named because the spots and flecks on the petals resemble speckled bird's eggs. They are currently available only as dwarf or miniature plants, but when the first specimens came on to the markets in the early 1900s, they were ordinary large zonal pelargoniums. They subsequently disappeared from sight for sixty years, until a

The miniature 'Urchin', another Formosa hybrid.

Pelargoniums are referred to as a group, this means that they belong to the Zonal type of plant. People began to apply themselves to cultivating fancyleafed pelargoniums in the 19th century. The English grower Peter Grieve played a major part in this. Not only did he develop a number of fancyleafed plants, he also wrote a handsome book with fine illustrations about them in 1850.

It was not altogether fortuitous that these plants were developed in Victorian times, when stylized flower beds and symmetrical forms were popular. Colourful foliage plants were just right for that formal kind of layout.

'Snowflake Atomic' – the foliage of some scented-leafed pelargoniums is also variegated.

'Golden Chalice' is a miniature with variegated leaves and speckled flowers – lovely for a windowsill.

The flowers of fancyleafed pelargoniums were – and are – often removed, because their colours are not always as fine as those of the foliage. Leaf development also benefits from this treatment.

How is variegated foliage created?

Variegated leaves are partly lacking in chlorophylls, which are used to convert light into food. Leaves without chlorophylls die because they do not have the ability carry out this conversion.

It sometimes happens that a green plant produces a shoot with leaves lacking in chlorophylls in some areas. This type of leaf will develop white or cream margins or blotches. Attempts may then be made to cultivate such a shoot separately to produce a plant with what is called 'silver'-variegated foliage.

Plants produce leaves in shades varying from very pale, even yellowish green, to dark green.

Above: 'Princess Alexandra' has an entirely white shoot.

'Miss Burdett Coutts', a lovely fancy-leafed pelargonium.

Pelargoniums also have a distinct red pigment in their foliage, and this appears as a dark zone, a ring or a blotch. It is possible to see the pigment with its own particular shade of red in areas where the leaf is partly white. The three shades of white, green and red may overlap to create other colours, and that is how the various groups of plants with variegated foliage are produced.

The following terms are commonly used:

- **Gold-variegated foliage** for yellow or yellow-green leaves;
- **Silver-variegated foliage** for green leaves with white or cream margins or blotches.
- **Tri-coloured foliage** for silver-variegated leaves with a coloured zone. The leaves of these plants have at least three colours: green, white, and brown or red.

Cultivation

Because pelargoniums with variegated leaves have a weak root system, they should not be planted in

'Contrast' has leaves coloured green, light yellow, red and brown.   *Below: the magnificent fancy-leafed 'Falkland's Hero'.*

excessively large pots or given too much fertilizer. Half the normal amount is enough. They may be kept at a slightly higher winter temperature than other Zonals. They can overwinter on a windowsill; the gold-variegated plants will do particularly well by a light window. In summer, the plants may be taken outdoors, as light and fresh air make them stronger. The lighter their position, the better the colours will develop, but hot afternoon sun is too much of a good thing.

'Monarch' has cream edges and blotches.

CHAPTER 4

Cultivation

If you wish to buy pelargoniums, it is easy enough to go along to the nearest garden centre, where you will find plenty of upright and trailing pelargoniums at a relatively low cost. You may well be able to buy a few Angels, a Stellar or two, and some scented-leafed specimens as well – enough to ensure a bright and colourful display all round the house throughout the summer.

If, however, you have become interested in the many unusual species, you will need to visit a specialized grower. The special kinds cannot be propagated as mass products, and the grower is therefore obliged to tend a number of parent plants over a long period in order to obtain a large amount of cuttings. The cuttings must be cultivated in heated greenhouses, where it is also essential to keep an eye on their health and avoid disease. Such labourintensive work is hardly compatible with modern conditions.

Fortunately, however, there are still a few growers who take pleasure in maintaining the range of special pelargoniums. It is also possible to join a Geranium and Pelargonium Society with members who collect species which even specialists have given up as too uneconomical to cultivate.

Colour and fragrance all round the house throughout the summer.

The pelargonium is now ready to begin a new season.

Nutrients

Aided by sunlight, the chlorophylls in a plant convert water into carbohydrates and enable the plant to grow. Light is therefore essential for the growth process. Plants also need food from the soil, the principal nutrients being:
– **nitrogen (N),** which is converted into the proteins that are essential to growth;

Left: Pelargonium *'Frank Headley'* has a good spread, and fills a pot nicely.

Right: Stellar *'Pixie Rose'*.

Below: Stellar *'Purple Heart'*, a rare specimen.

– **phosphorus (P),** which is important for root formation;
– **potassium (K),** which helps the plant to build up a resistance to disease.
The NPK is normally stated on packets of fertilizer. NPK 4+5+6, for instance, means that

Zonal pelargonium 'Platinum'.

the fertilizer contains 4% nitrogen, 5% phosphorus, and 6% potassium. A fourth figure indicating the percentage of magnesium is sometimes provided as well (magnesium, for instance, is a component of dolomite). In addition to these substances, plants also need trace elements, which occur in sufficient quantities in good soil. As pots can contain only limited amounts of soil, and nutrients may be washed away by water, you start adding plant food about four to six weeks after repotting.

Natural and artificial fertilizers

Firstly, there are organic fertilizers, natural substances such as farmyard manure, blood and bone meal.

Some are available in composite form for container plants, with the NPK and instructions for use provided by the manufacturer. Then there are inorganic or artificial fertilizers. Some of the many brands only mention whether they are intended for foliage or flowering plants, whereas others also state the NPK. I myself prefer the latter variety, as I do not want to use fertilizers with the same composition throughout the year. A fertilizer with a slightly greater nitrogen content, for example, is only suitable for pelargoniums in early spring, when the plant needs to produce a lot of new foliage. It is better to use a fertilizer with a low nitrogen content for the rest of the year to prevent the plants outgrowing their strength.

Fertilizers with a long period of activity are convenient. They include Osmocote, a fertilizer consisting of granules which release nutrients very slowly, depending on the temperature and amount of water. The recommended quantity of granules is mixed with the soil in spring, and no further attention is required throughout the summer.

This kind of fertilizer is rather more expensive than the others.

Stellar 'Golden Ears'.

'Elmsett' bears double flowers and belong to the Bird's Egg group.

Amount of fertilizer

Never exceed the recommended quantities, as too much fertilizer will damage the roots. Some plants, including the large Zonals and ivy-leafed pelargoniums, have big appetites. The scented-leafed varieties need rather less food, and the dwarf and minisure plants should never be given more than half the amount shown on the packet. Start giving the plants fertilizer in spring, four to six weeks after potting on, and continue until August. The plants subsequently need to stop growing and to harden off before their period of rest in winter. This does not apply to plants that you want to keep in a livingroom in winter. They will continue to grow slowly and therefore need feeding, although far less frequently than before. Instead of once a week, for example, once a month would be enough.

'Pink Rosebud' is a hungry plant.

Above: Ivy-leafed 'Maya'.

Left: 'Coronia' a zonal pelargonium with furled petals.

Right: Ivy-leafed pelargonium 'Blanche Roche'.

Below: Ivy-leafed pelargonium 'Le Pirat'.

The miniature 'Royal Norfolk' dislikes very wet soil.

on a saucer. Pour off any remaining water half an hour later. The cooler the plants are kept in winter, the less water they will require.

Overwintering

If you do not have a frostfree greenhouse or cool conservatory, you should use your imagination to find a suitable place for pelar-goniums to overwinter. Temperatures from 5-10ºC (41-50ºF) and a light space which can be aired regularly are ideal.

Pelargoniums do not become very dormant, and begin to grow again if the temperature rises above 10ºC (50ºF). If their location is too dark at that time, stems will grow into long, lax, light-coloured tendrils. Fortunately, that situation

Angel 'Moon Maiden' will tolerate a wet summer.

'Dwarf Miriam Baisey'.

can be rectified. When repotting the plants in early spring, cut back the long shoots and trim them into an attractive shape. This is the time to put the plants in a light place and gradually raise the temperature. Unfortunately, some problems may occur at this time. People are often advised to overwinter pelargoniums in an attic or a cellar, areas which are fairly dark in many houses. Provided they are well cared for, it is possible to leave them there for one or two months, but where do you put them in February/March, when they are beginning to sprout? You might put them out of doors from the beginning of April, but they should be taken indoors again in the evening. Never put them

'Crowfield' is a miniature with large pink flowers.

out of doors in March, when it is still far too cold. All these matters should be considered if you decide to overwinter your pelargoniums in too dark a place.

In the livingroom

If kept indoors, it is best for pelargoniums to overwinter close to a welllit window. A light hall or staircase would be very suitable. The same applies to bedrooms, where it is usually much cooler than in a livingroom. Even so, there are several pelargoniums that can simply overwinter in a livingroom or a kitchen, provided there is not a radiator under the window. If there is one, the windowsill should be wide enough for the plants not to be affected by direct heat. Zonal pelargoniums are the most suitable kinds for keeping in a livingroom, especially the miniatures and fancyleafed varieties, which do not mind a slightly warmer situation. Even the Stellars and

Miniature zonal pelargonium 'Altair'.

Stellar 'Vectis Gold'.

Left: A Pelargonium cucullatum *hybrid next to* Agave Americana *'Variegata' in a greenhouse.*

Next pages: A safe haven for the winter.

larger Zonals will survive the winter in those conditions. They will continue to grow, and may even flower. If they flower, the plants will need regular watering and and some extra food from time to time. As for tolerance, some of the scented-leafed plants might well be kept in a livingroom, but they are not always good enough to look at all day while dormant.

The plants that you would like to overwinter in a livingroom should be taken indoors before the central heating is switched on, say in early September, to avoid too extreme a transition. Angels and Regals need a cold period lasting from four to six weeks if they are to flower well the following year. Leave them out of doors until the first night frost, and then find a cool place for them. They may gradually be given a warmer location from February onwards.

When pruning is inadvisable
It is better not to prune pelargoniums that you have moved indoors in autumn, as pruning will stimulate new growth at a time when the plants are supposed to have a period of rest.

Of course, it is all right to tidy them up a little and to remove a few protruding branches so that they will take up less space.

Wherever your pelargoniums are to spend the winter, they should not be forgotten. Let them have some fresh air whenever possible, though not when it is frosty. Remove yellowed leaves, and water moderately depending on the temperature.

CHAPTER 5

Dwarf 'Susan Payne'.

Miniature 'Pink Splendor'.

Miniature 'Michèle'.

Miniature 'Candy'

Above: Deacon 'Romance' branches out without encouragement.

Below: Dwarf ivy-leafed pelargonium 'Pink Gay Baby'.   *Right: Zonal pelargonium 'Honeywood's Matthew'.*

Dwarf pelargonium 'Rusty'.

Below: This stellar has a bacterial disease. The black spot where there used to be a leaf is clearly visible.

and below flower buds. Remove them by hand, or by holding the plant under the tap. This will often keep an entire plague of aphids in check.

Whitefly

Whitefly often causes a lot of trouble, especially in greenhouses. All you need do is brush past a plant, and a cloud of insects flies out of it. The eggs are left behind. Hold the plant under a tap and rinse them off the underside of the leaves. This will help to control the plague to some extent. The insects themselves can only be rinsed off under the tap if it is so cold that when you lift up the pot they remain where they are as if they were petrified. *Pelargonium* x *domesticum,* the Regal pelargonium, is particularly subject to infestation with whitefly, one of the reasons why some people do not like having the plant. You may also turn this problem to your advantage by using *P.* x *domesticum* as bait in your greenhouse. A fuchsia may be used for the same purpose, as whitefly prefers

Keep to a particular group, or switch to different species from time to time. Space between the plants will benefit their health!

Time

Time is another factor you will need to consider. You should inspect your plants regularly to discover undesirable developments in good time. A genuine enthusiast usually enjoys pottering about among the plants, and does not bother too much about the time it takes. Remove yellow leaves in good time: in our damp climate they soon become a breeding-ground for moulds.

Grey Mould

Take a good look at the plants when removing yellow leaves. If you see a grey substance between the leaves, you've been warned. It may be mould caused by damp and by the plants being too close together.

If you remove any affected leaves straight away and allow the plant more space, it will soon recover.

Rust

Grey spots on the upperside of leaves, and round brown spots on the underside are signs of

Ivy-leafed 'Blizzard'.

'Bridesmaid', a dwarf zonal with golden-green foliage.

Pelargonium peltatum.

rust. Remove affected leaves carefully. If you have been quick to discover the fungus, removing leaves once or twice more may be enough. This will usually prevent the plant being affected everywhere.

'Wedding Royale' is a dwarf Rosebud.

Ivy-leafed pelargonium 'Rio Grande'.

Stem rot

If (part of) a stem turns black, it is probably affected by stem rot. Cut out the black section and check whether the rootball is too wet. If it is, roll it in kitchen paper to dry (see Chapter 4, Cultivation).

Lumpy leaves

Lumps on the foliage may be caused by a virus. There is no simple solution to this problem. A plant may recover over a period of time.
Remove the affected leaves and give the plant a little extra care. All you can do is hope it will recover.

Aphids

Aphids impede a plant's growth. Tips are devoured, leaves curl and develop lumps. The whole plant becomes sticky as a result of the honeydew deposits given off by the insects. Aphids are usually to be found at growing points

Dwarf pelargonium 'Rusty'.

Below: This stellar has a bacterial disease. The black spot where there used to be a leaf is clearly visible.

and below flower buds. Remove them by hand, or by holding the plant under the tap. This will often keep an entire plague of aphids in check.

Whitefly

Whitefly often causes a lot of trouble, especially in greenhouses. All you need do is brush past a plant, and a cloud of insects flies out of it. The eggs are left behind. Hold the plant under a tap and rinse them off the underside of the leaves. This will help to control the plague to some extent. The insects themselves can only be rinsed off under the tap if it is so cold that when you lift up the pot they remain where they are as if they were petrified. *Pelargonium* x *domesticum*, the Regal pelargonium, is particularly subject to infestation with whitefly, one of the reasons why some people do not like having the plant. You may also turn this problem to your advantage by using *P.* x *domesticum* as bait in your greenhouse. A fuchsia may be used for the same purpose, as whitefly prefers

fuchsias to pelargoniums. Checking and cleaning up a fuchsia every day takes less time than checking all the other plants.

Spraying

If pests get out of hand in spite of the above measures, it is always possible to use other methods.

Avoid dangerous chemicals if at all possible, and use environment-friendly remedies instead. Any garden centre will give advice on the subject.

Bacterial disease

All pelargoniums are susceptible to bacterial disease. Unfortunately, the disease is hardly recognizable.

The plant's leaves turn yellow, but that may have many other causes. If you were to throw away every pelargonium with yellow leaves, none would be left.

Experienced growers can sometimes recognize the disease. There may be a minute black spot at the base of the leaf stem, and leaves may develop black veins.

Often, however, the plant will be dead before the symptoms appear. It may decline and die very quickly. The causes are often circumstances which may cause stress in plants, very high temperatures for instance. Fortunately, it is unusual to buy a plant suffering from a bacterial disease. Growers have a keen eye for symptoms, naturally so, as it would be a disaster if this infectious disease were to occur in their propagating houses.

If you do have a pelargonium that dies suddenly for no apparent reason, disinfect and clean its pot and also the place where it has been kept. You would obviously not throw the plant on to the compost heap. All you can do is hope that other plants will not be affected.

Pelargonium x domesticum is subject to infestation by whitefly.

CHAPTER 6

In and around the House, on the Patio, and in the Garden

We buy plants to adorn our house, or patio, or garden. We take a critical look at possible locations, and try to imagine what the plants intended for them will look like there. That, at least, is how it should be, but usually it is the other way round. We buy a plant because we admire it, and then look for somewhere to put it. At least, that is what regularly happens to me. When I had only just discovered pelargoniums, I felt an urge to buy a fancy-leafed specimen, a genuine one, with shades of green,white, red, and bronze. I could imagine it in all its glory by the front door – well cared for and in bright sunlight. Of course I could not rest until I had obtained a cutting. I tended it lovingly until it had grown into a handsome plant, and carried out of doors triumphantly in May. And then I began lugging it from place to place, but there was not a single spot where it showed up to perfection. My garden simply is not right for such an ornamental plant. I gave it away to someone with a more appropriate setting for it, and now I just admire that kind of pelargonium in other people's gardens. The more colourful, striking, and exotic a plant is, the more difficult it may be to find a suitable place for it.

A wall covered in ivy-leafed pelargoniums.

Ivy-leafed 'Kelly'.

long, straggling shoots and just a few flowers. Ivy-leafed pelargoniums also look lovely growing through the branches of a climbing rose. When the rose is having a few weeks rest, the blooms

Left: Scented-leafed pelargoniums look lovely in a herb garden.

Below: Ivy-leafed pelargoniums covering a wall on La Palma.

will enliven the greenery and appear to shorten the wait for the rose's next flowering.

Finally – plant a few scented-leafed pelargoniums in your herb garden, a place where they really look at home.

Above: 'Greengold Petit Pièrce' has dark green butterfly markings on yellow-green foliage.

Below: Zonal pelargonium 'Distinction', with a narrow black zone along the edges of its leaves.

Further Reading

Harold Bagust, *Miniature and Dwarf Geraniums (Pelargoniums),* 1988, Christopher Helm, London

D. Clifford, *Pelargoniums including the popular Geranium,* 1970, Blanford Press Ltd, Chatham

Rita Scheen-Prins, *Alles over Geraniums (Pelargoniums)* (All about Geraniums (Pelargoniums), 1982, Gaade, Amerongen

Jan Taylor, *Pelargoniums for Colour and Variety,* 1990, The Crowood Press.

J.J.D. vd Walt, *Pelargoniums of Southern Africa I,* 1977, Purnell & Sons, Cape Town.

J.J.A. vd Walt and P.J. Vorster, *Pelargoniums of Southern Africa II,* 1981, Juta & Co, Cape Town.

J.J.A. vd Walt and P.J. Vorster, *Pelargoniums of Southern Africa III,* 1988, National Botanic Gardens, Kirstenbosch.

Acknowledgements

The publishers and author wish to thank the following individuals for their kind help in creating this book:

The Grijsen family, Winterswijk
Mrs Van de Hoek, Heino
Mr Theo Jeukens of the Fuchsiakwekerij Jeukens (Jeukens Fuchsia Nursery), Ambt Delden
The Metz family, Nes, Ameland

Index